FINGERPICKING ACOUSTIC CLASSICS

ISBN 978-1-4950-6427-2

HAL•LEONARD®

7777 W. BLUEMOUND RD. P.O. BOX 13819 MILWAUKEE, WI 53213

INTRODUCTION TO FINGERSTYLE GUITAR

Fingerstyle (a.k.a. fingerpicking) is a guitar technique that means you literally pick the strings with your right-hand fingers and thumb. This contrasts with the conventional technique of strumming and playing single notes with a pick (a.k.a. flatpicking). For fingerpicking, you can use any type of guitar: acoustic steel-string, nylon-string classical, or electric.

THE RIGHT HAND

The most common right-hand position is shown here.

Use a high wrist; arch your palm as if you were holding a ping-pong ball. Keep the thumb outside and away from the fingers, and let the fingers do the work rather than lifting your whole hand.

The thumb generally plucks the bottom strings with downstrokes on the left side of the thumb and thumbnail. The other fingers pluck the higher strings using upstrokes with the fleshy tip of the fingers and fingernails. The thumb and fingers should pluck one string per stroke and not brush over several strings.

Another picking option you may choose to use is called hybrid picking (a.k.a. plectrum-style fingerpicking). Here, the pick is usually held between the thumb and first finger, and the three remaining fingers are assigned to pluck the higher strings.

THE LEFT HAND

The left-hand fingers are numbered 1 through 4.

Be sure to keep your fingers arched, with each joint bent; if they flatten out across the strings, they will deaden the sound when you fingerpick. As a general rule, let the strings ring as long as possible when playing fingerstyle.

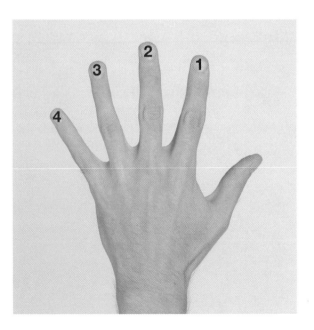

Ain't No Sunshine

Words and Music by Bill Withers

3

long an - y - time___ she goes a - way.

𝄋 Verse

2. Won - der this ___ time where she's gone;
gone,

won - der if _____ she's gone to stay.)
on - ly dark - ness ev - 'ry day.)

Ain't no sun - shine when she's gone, _____ and this house _ just ain't no

To Coda

home an - y - time _____ she goes a - way.

Bridge

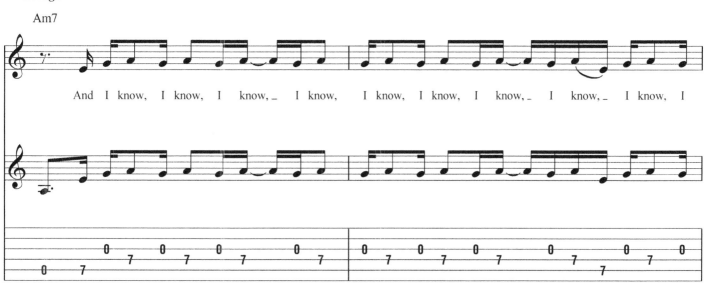

And I know, I know, I know, _ I know, I know, I know, I know, _ I know, _ I know, I

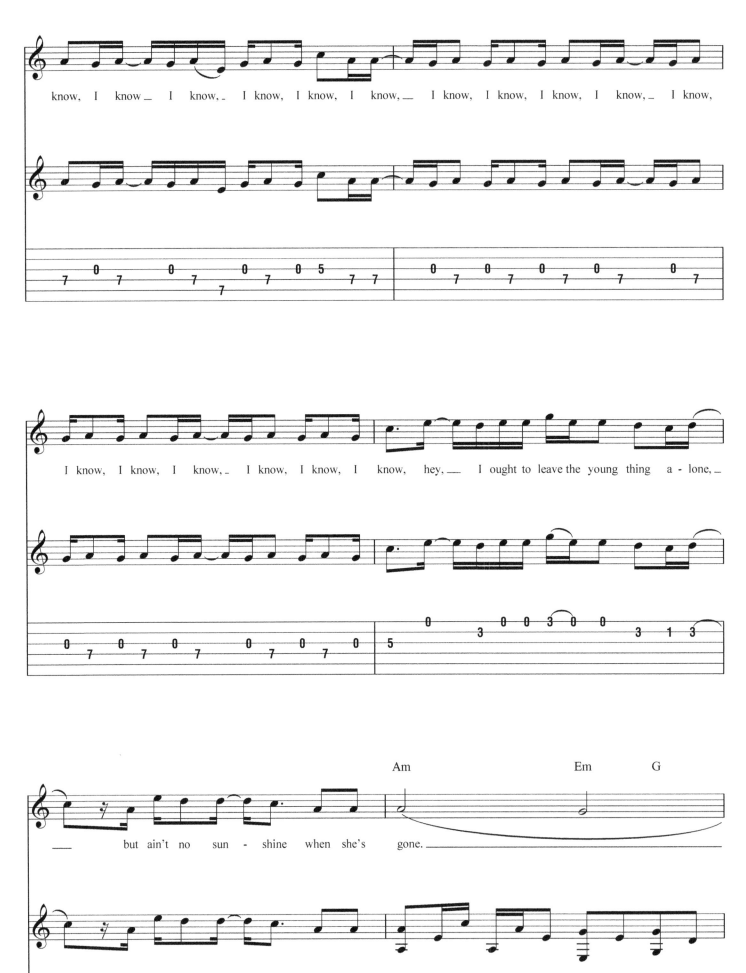

know, I know _ I know, _ I know, I know, I know, _ I know, I know, I know, I know, _ I know,

I know, I know, I know, _ I know, I know, I know, hey, _ I ought to leave the young thing a - lone, _

_ but ain't no sun - shine when she's gone. _

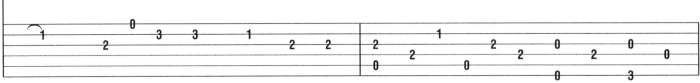

D.S. al Coda

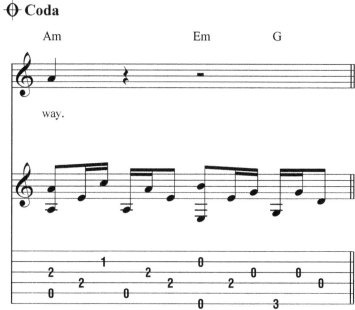

Outro

An - y - time ___ she goes a - way.

An - y - time ___ she goes a - way.

Blackbird

Words and Music by John Lennon and Paul McCartney

you were on - ly wait - ing for this
you were on - ly wait - ing for this

mo - ment to a - rise.

mo - ment to be free.

% Chorus

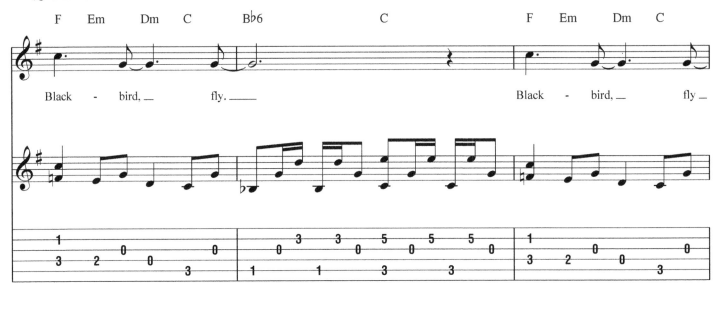

Black - bird, __ fly. __   Black - bird, __ fly __

To Coda 1 ⊕

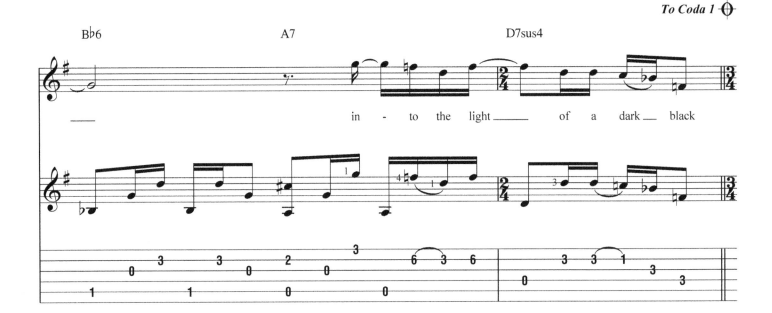

__   in - to the light __ of a dark __ black

Interlude

night.

10

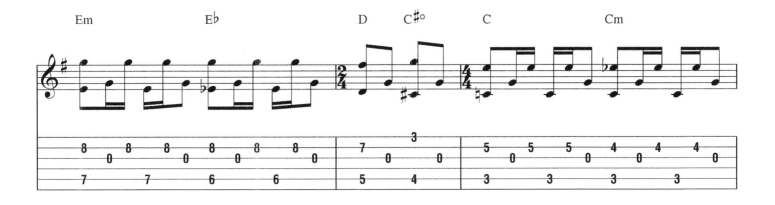

D.S. al Coda 1

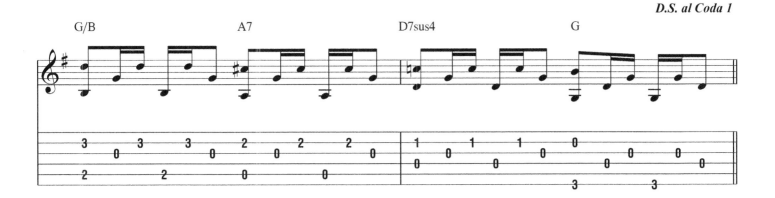

 **Coda 1**

Interlude

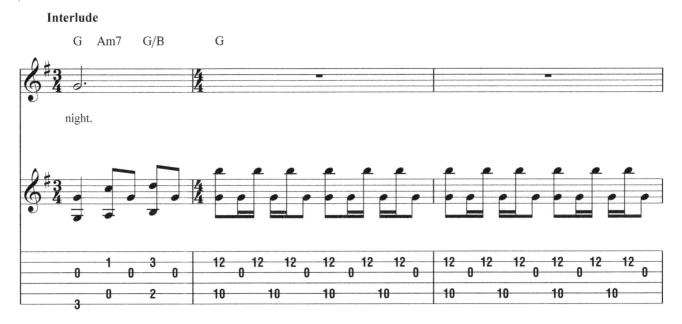

night.

D.S.S. al Coda 2

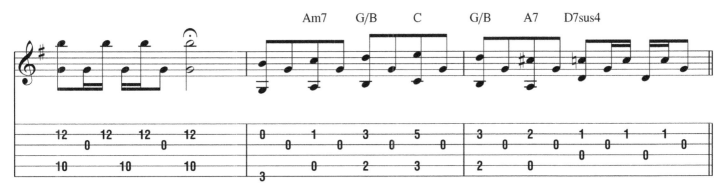

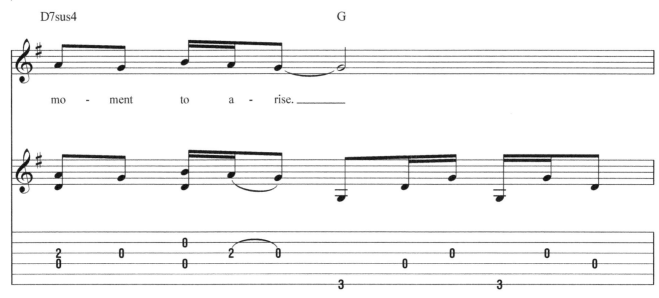

mo - ment to a - rise. _____

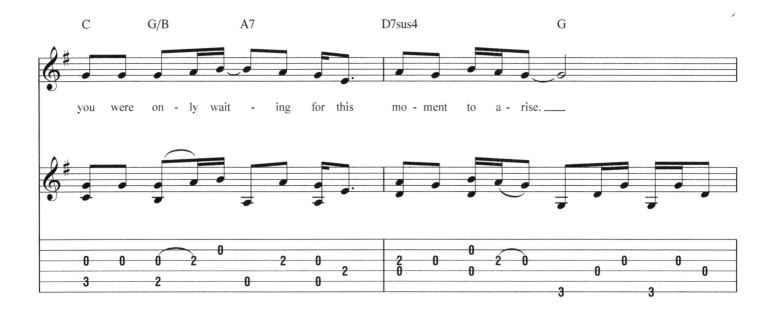

you were on - ly wait - ing for this mo - ment to a - rise. ___

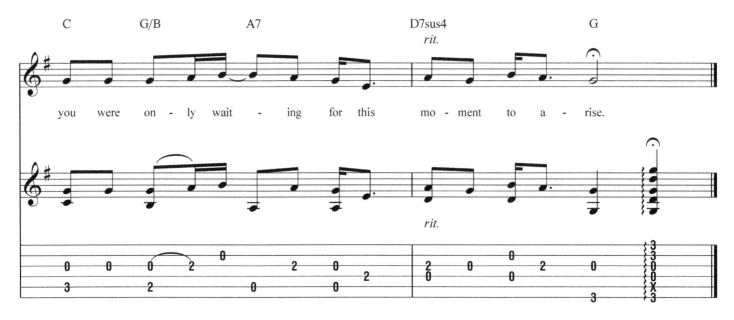

you were on - ly wait - ing for this mo - ment to a - rise.

For What It's Worth

Words and Music by Stephen Stills

Intro
Moderately

Verse

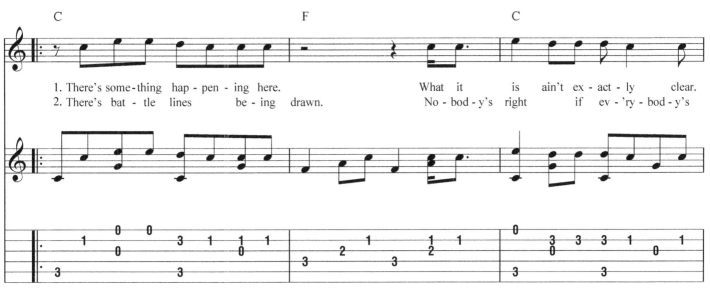

1. There's some-thing hap-pen-ing here. What it is ain't ex-act-ly clear.
2. There's bat-tle lines be-ing drawn. No-bod-y's right if ev-'ry-bod-y's

wrong. There's a man with a gun o-ver there tell-ing
Young peo-ple speak-ing their minds, get-ting

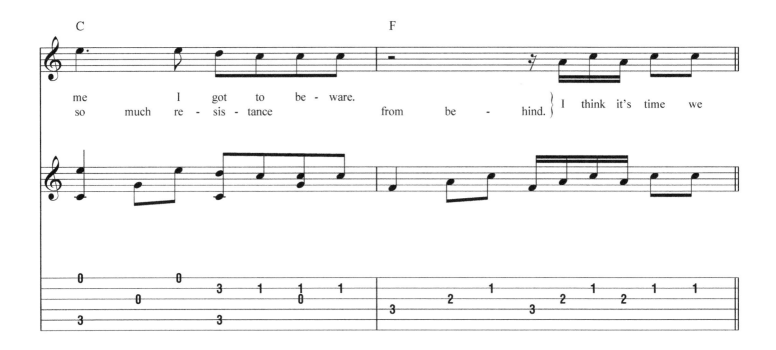

me   I got to be-ware.

so much re - sis - tance   from be - hind.   } I think it's time we

𝄋 Chorus

stop,   child - ren, what's that sound? __ Ev - 'ry - bod - y look what's go - ing down. __

To Coda

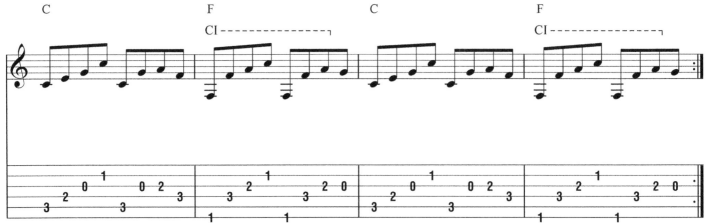

Verse

3. What a field day for the heat, a thou-sand peo-ple in the street sing-ing songs and car-ry-ing signs. Most-ly

D.S. al Coda ⊕ **Coda**

Verse

say, "Hoo-ray for our side." It's time we

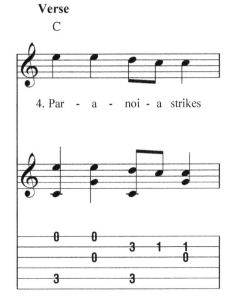

4. Par - a - noi - a strikes

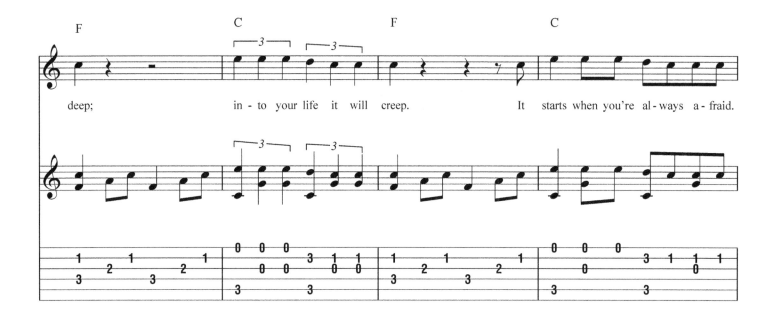

deep;   in - to your life it will creep.   It starts when you're al - ways a - fraid.

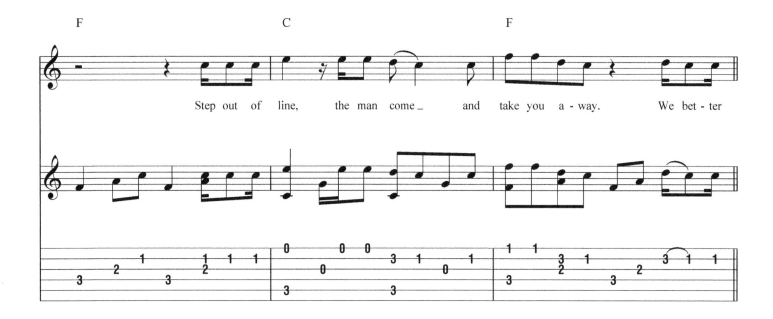

Step out of line,   the man come _   and take you a - way.   We bet - ter

Chorus

stop, hey, ___ what's that sound? _ Ev - 'ry - bod - y look what's go - ing, we bet - ter

stop, hey, what's that sound? __ Ev- 'ry-bod - y look what's go - ing, we bet - ter

stop, child - ren, what's that sound? __ Ev- 'ry - bod - y look what's go - ing down. __

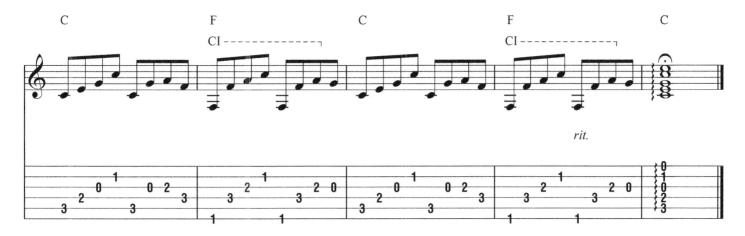

Can't Find My Way Home

Words and Music by Steve Winwood

Intro

Moderately slow

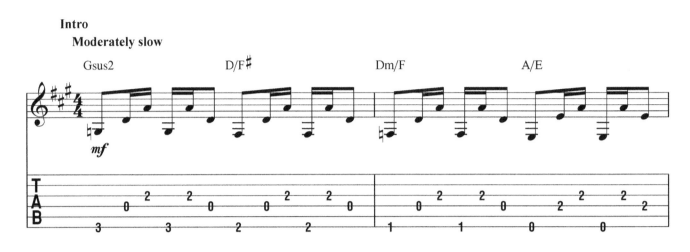

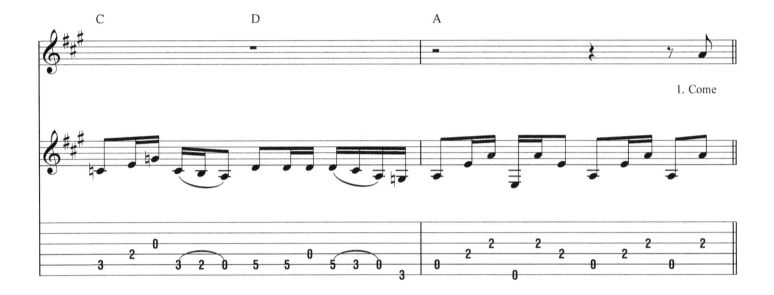

1. Come

Verse

down off___ your throne___ and leave your bod - y a - lone;
down on___ your own___ and leave your bod - y a - lone;

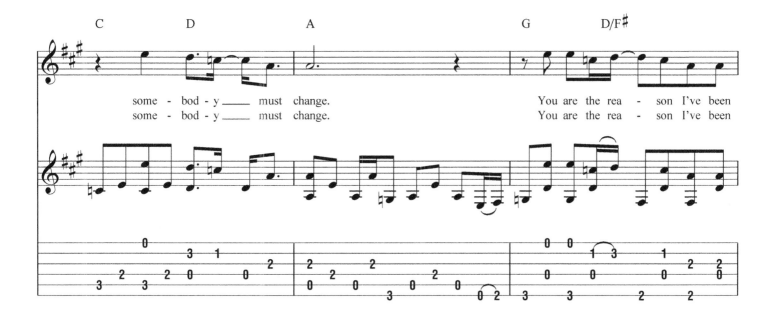

some - bod - y_____ must change. You are the rea - son I've been
some - bod - y_____ must change. You are the rea - son I've been

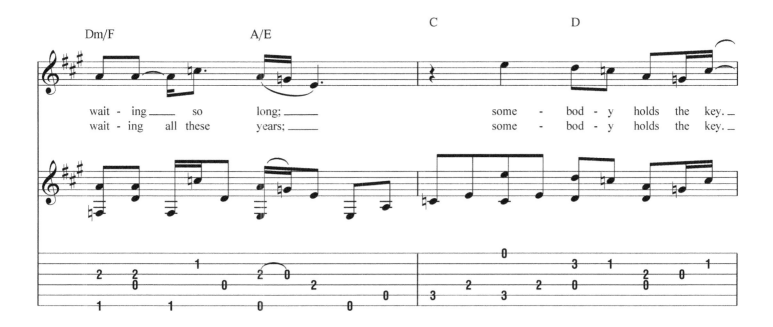

wait - ing_____ so long;_____ some - bod - y holds the key._
wait - ing all these years; _____ some - bod - y holds the key._

Chorus

Well, I'm _____ near the end _____ and I just _____ ain't got _____ the time, _

and I'm ___ wast - ed ___ and I can't ___ find my way ___ home. ___

Interlude

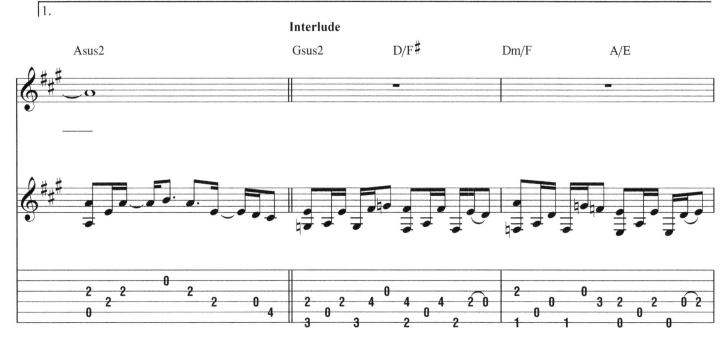

2. Come home.

Outro

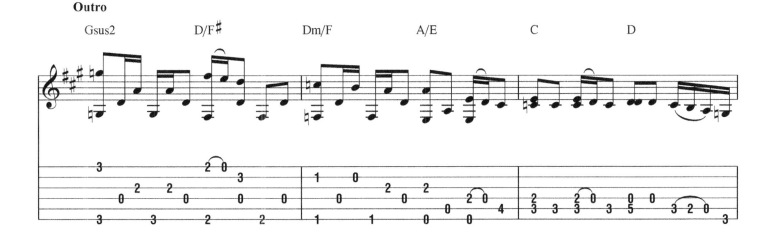

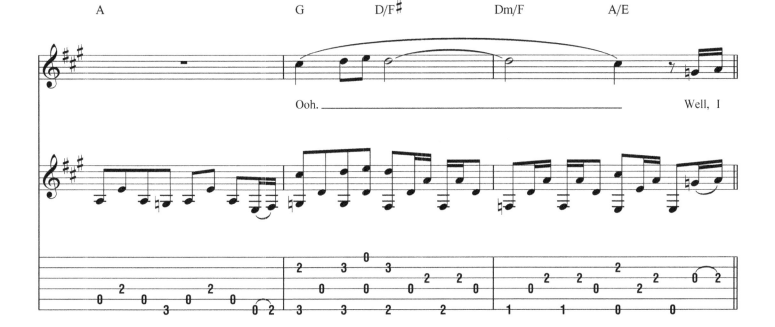

Ooh. _____ Well, I

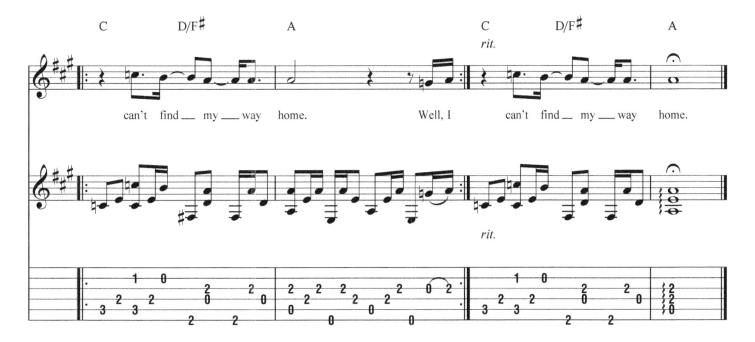

can't find __ my __ way home.   Well, I   can't find __ my __ way home.

rit.

Catch the Wind

Words and Music by Donovan Leitch

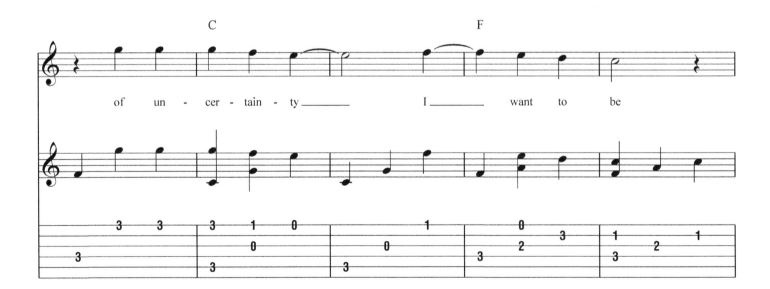

in the warm _____ hold of your lov - ing mind. ___

Verse

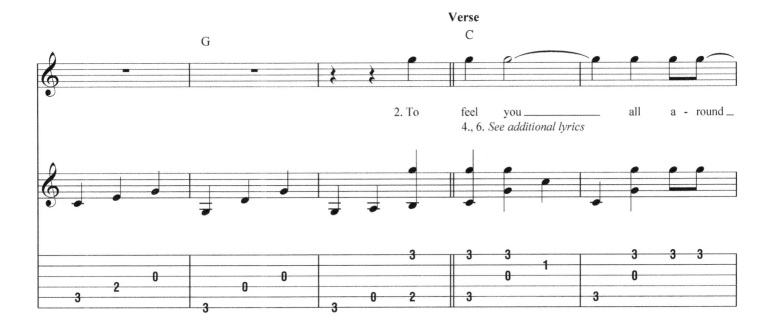

2. To feel you _____ all a - round ___
4., 6. See additional lyrics

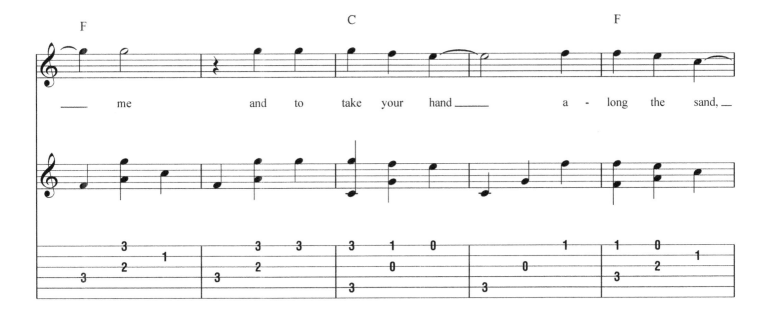

____ me and to take your hand _____ a - long the sand, ___

ah, but I may ___ as well try and catch the wind. ___

To Coda

___

3. When

Bridge

Did - dy, dee, dee, ___ did - dy, did - dy, ___ did - dy, did - dy, ___

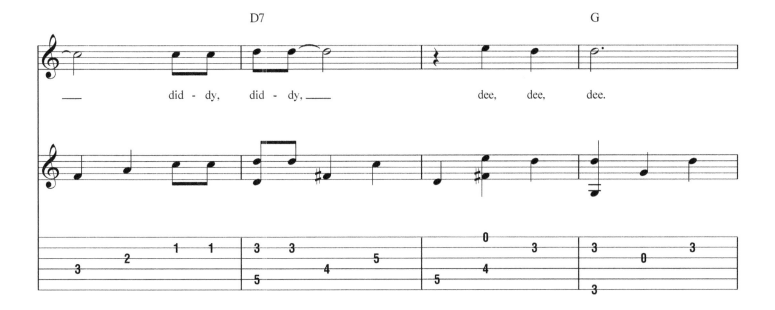

did - dy,   did - dy, ___   dee,   dee,   dee.

D.S. al Coda   **⊕ Coda**

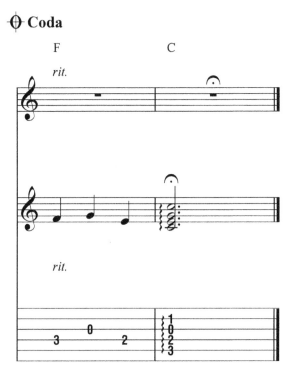

When

Additional Lyrics

3. When sundown pales the sky,
   I want to hide a while behind your smile,
   And everwhere I'd look, your eyes I'd find.

4. For me to love you now
   Would be the sweetest thing, t'would make me sing.
   Ah, but I may as well try and catch the wind.

5. When rain has hung the leaves with tears,
   I want you near to kill my fears,
   To help me leave all my blues behind.

6. For standing in your heart
   Is where I want to be and long to be.
   Ah, but I may as well try and catch the wind.

Fire and Rain

Words and Music by James Taylor

Intro
Moderately slow

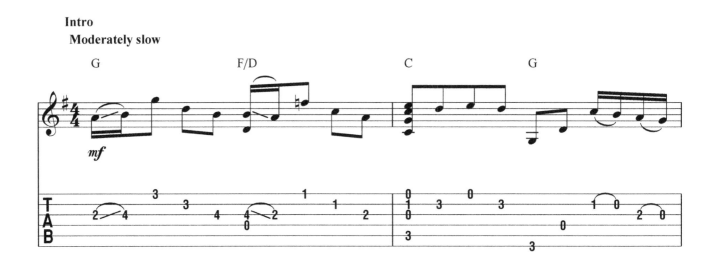

Verse

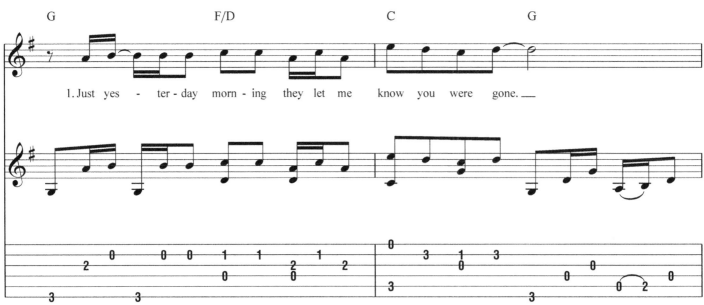

1. Just yes - ter-day morn-ing they let me know you were gone. __

Coda 🎯

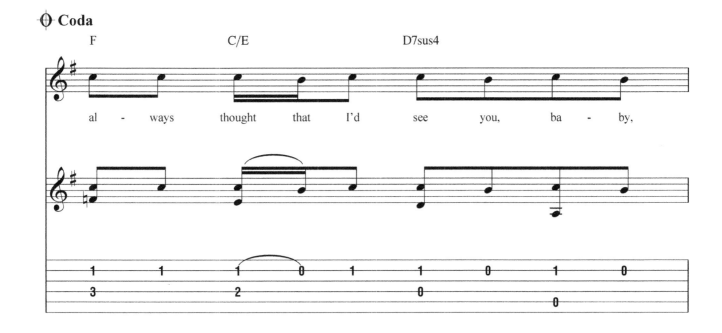

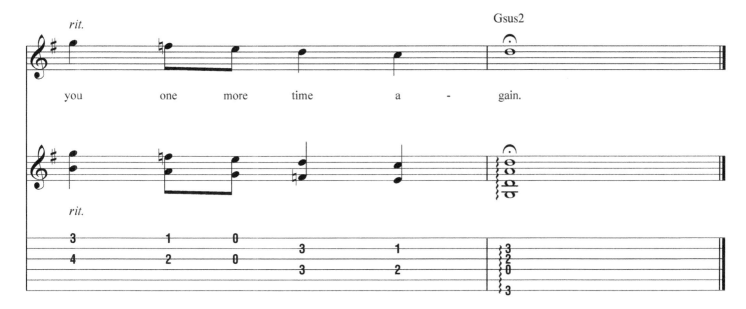

Free Fallin'

Words and Music by Tom Petty and Jeff Lynne

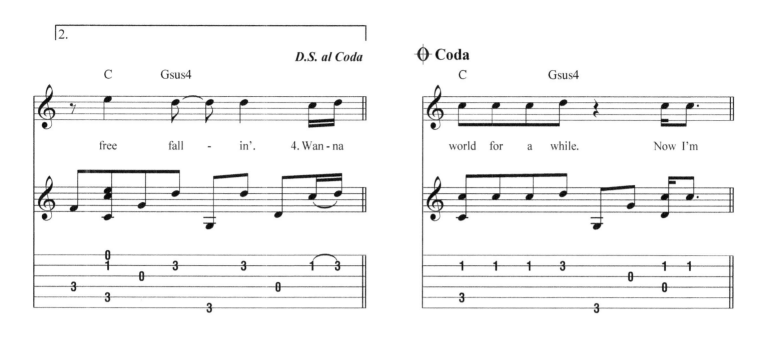

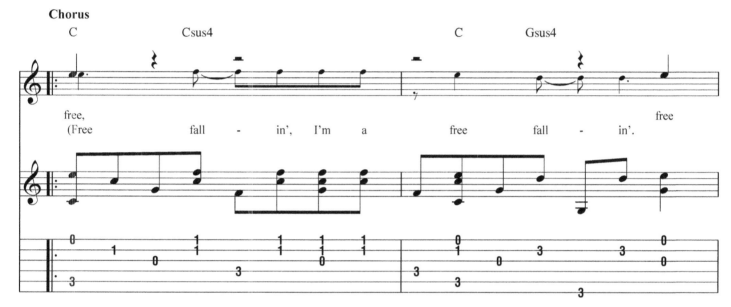

Additional Lyrics

2. It's a long day living in Reseda.
   There's a freeway running through the yard.
   And I'm a bad boy 'cause I don't even miss her.
   I'm a bad boy for breaking her heart.

3. And all the Vampires walking through the valley
   Move west down Ventura Boulevard.
   And all the bad boys are standing in the shadows.
   And the good girls are home with broken hearts.

4. Wanna glide down over Mulholland.
   I wanna write her name in the sky.
   I wanna free fall out into nothing.
   Gonna leave this world for a while.

Have You Ever Seen the Rain?

Words and Music by John Fogerty

1. Some-one told me long a - go
2. Yes - ter - day and days be - fore,

there's a calm be - fore the storm. I know, and
sun is cold and rain is hard. I know;

it's been com - ing for some time.
been that way for all my time.

When it's o - ver, so _____ they say, ___ it - 'll rain a sun -
'Til for - ev - er, on _____ it goes ___ through the cir - cle, fast _

- ny day. __ I know, _ shin - ing down _ like wa - ter.
___ and slow. _ I know; _ and it can't stop, _ I won - der.

Chorus

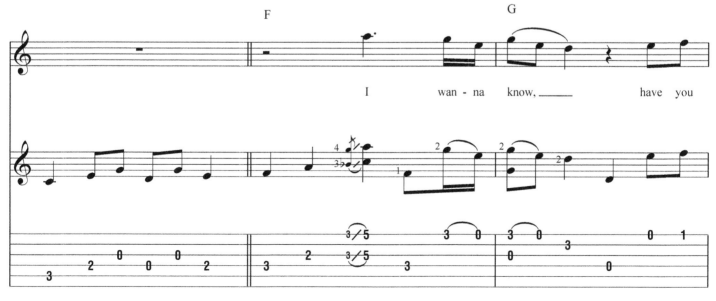

I wan - na know, _____ have you

ev - er   seen   the   rain?   I   wan - na

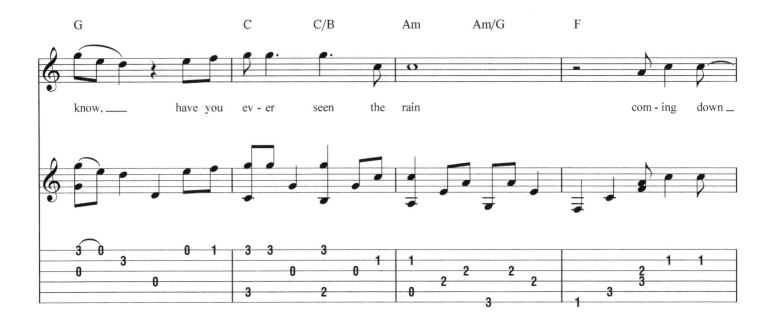

know, ___   have you   ev - er   seen   the   rain   com - ing   down ___

___   on   a   sun - ny   day? ___

Hotel California

Words and Music by Don Henley, Glenn Frey and Don Felder

Intro
Moderately slow

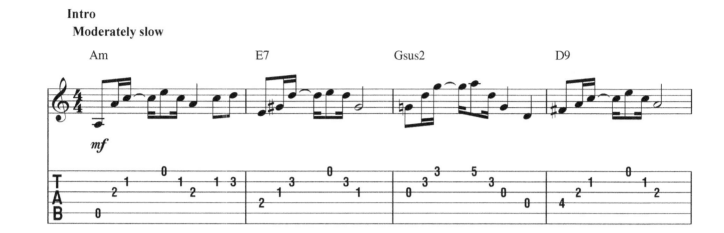

1. On a dark des-ert high-way, cool wind in my hair,
3. Her mind is Tif-fa-ny twist-ed, she got the Mer-ce-des bends.
5. Mir-rors on the ceil-ing, the pink cham-pagne on ice, and she said,

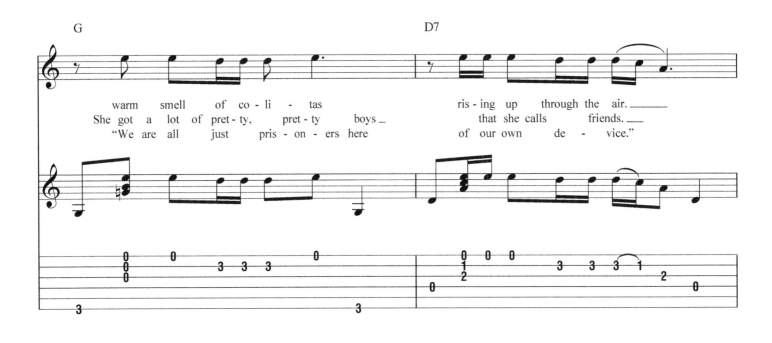

warm smell of co - li - tas   ris - ing up through the air. _____
She got a lot of pret - ty, pret - ty boys _   that she calls   friends. _____
"We are all   just   pris - on - ers here   of our own   de - vice."

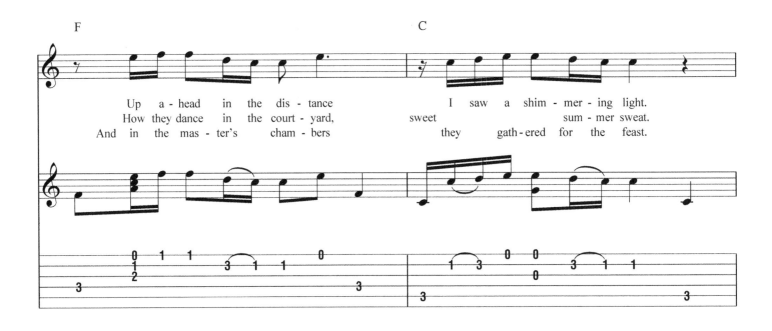

Up a - head in the dis - tance   I saw a shim - mer - ing light.
How they dance in the court - yard,   sweet   sum - mer sweat.
And in the mas - ter's   cham - bers   they gath - ered for the feast.

My head grew heav - y and my sight grew dim; ___   I had to stop   for the night.
Some   dance   to re - mem - ber;   some   dance   to for - get.
They   stab   it   with their ___ steel - y knives but they just   can't   kill the beast.

Verse

2. There she stood in the door-way; I heard the mis-sion bell.
4. So, I called up the cap-tain, "Please bring me my ___ wine." He said that,
6. Last thing I re-mem-ber I was run-ning ___ for the door. ___

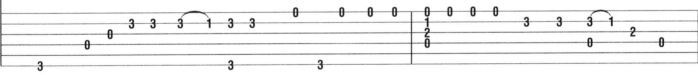

I was think-ing to my-self ___ this could be heav-en or this could be hell. ___
"We have-n't had that spir-it here ___ since nine-teen six-ty nine." ___
I had to find the pas-sage back ___ to the place I was be-fore. ___

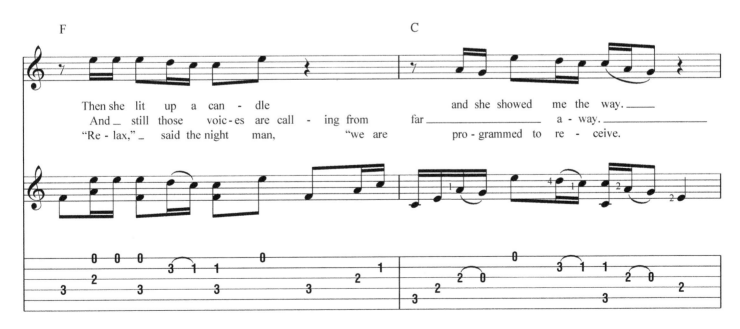

Then she lit up a can-dle and she showed me the way. ___
And ___ still those voic-es are call-ing from far ___ a-way. ___
"Re-lax," ___ said the night man, "we are pro-grammed to re-ceive.

To Coda ⊕

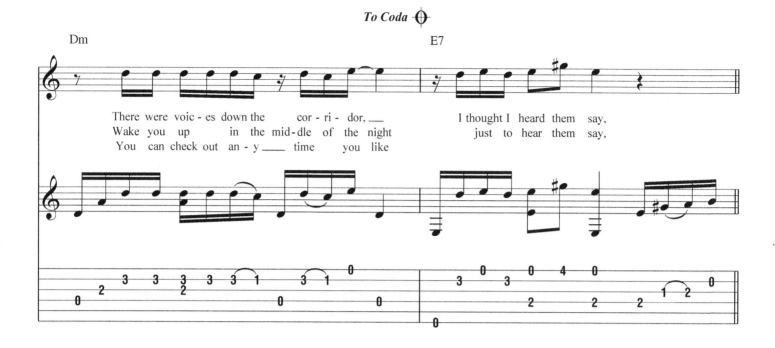

There were voic - es down the cor - ri - dor, __ I thought I heard them say,
Wake you up in the mid - dle of the night just to hear them say,
You can check out an - y __ time you like

Chorus

"Wel - come __ to the Ho - tel Cal - i - for - nia, such a

love - ly place, __ such a love - ly face. __

F
C

Plen-ty of room ___ at the Ho-tel Cal - i - for - nia.
Liv-ing it up ___ at the Ho-tel Cal - i - for - nia.

An - y
What a

[1.

Dm
E7

time of year ___
nice sur - prise, ___

you can find it here." ___
bring your

[2.

D.S. al Coda

⊕ **Coda**

E7
E7

al - i - bis." ___

but you can ___ nev - er leave."

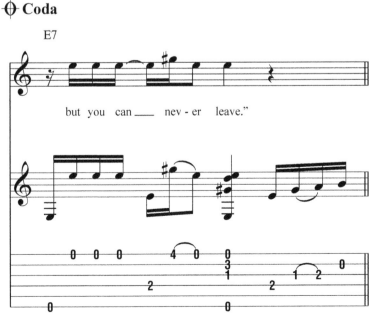

Outro

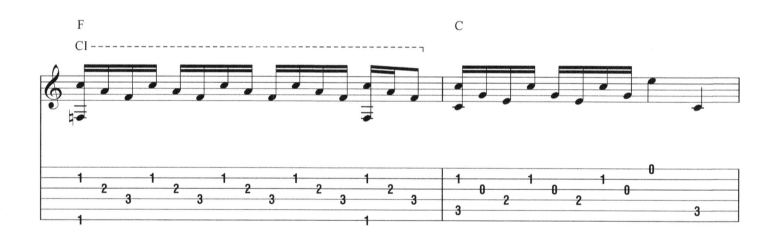

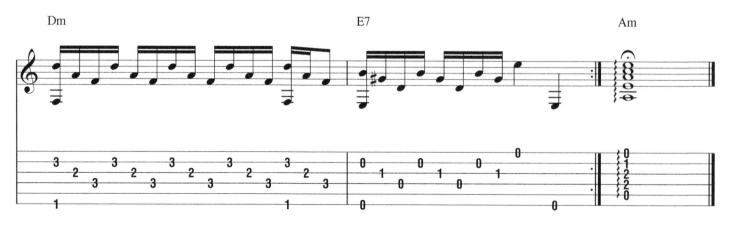

44

The Joker

Words and Music by Steve Miller, Eddie Curtis and Ahmet Ertegun

speak   of the Pom - pa - tus   of   love. ____

Verse

2. Peo - ple talk ___ a - bout ___ me, ba - by;
3., 5. *See additional lyrics*

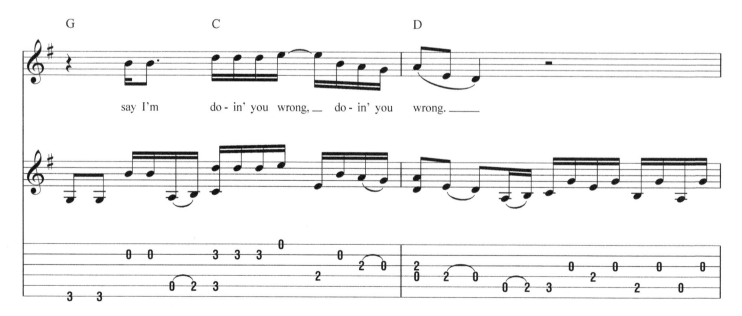

say I'm   do - in' you wrong, ___ do - in' you   wrong. ____

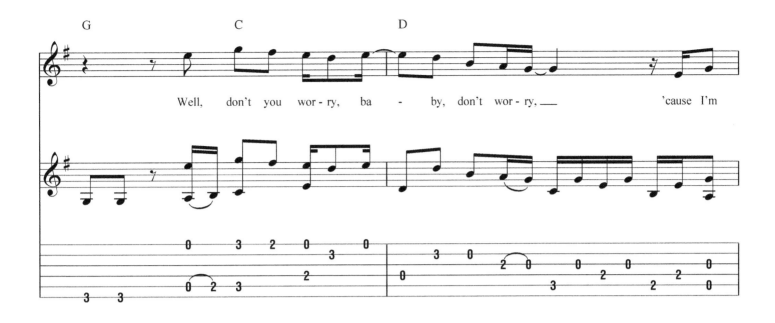

Well, don't you wor - ry, ba - by, don't wor - ry, ___ 'cause I'm

right here, right here, right here, right here at home. ___ 'Cause I'm a

Chorus

pick - er, I'm a grin - ner, I'm a lov - er, and I'm a sin - ner.

I play my mu - sic in ___ the sun. _____ I'm a

jok - er, I'm a smok - er, I'm a mid - night ___ tok - er.

To Coda ⊕

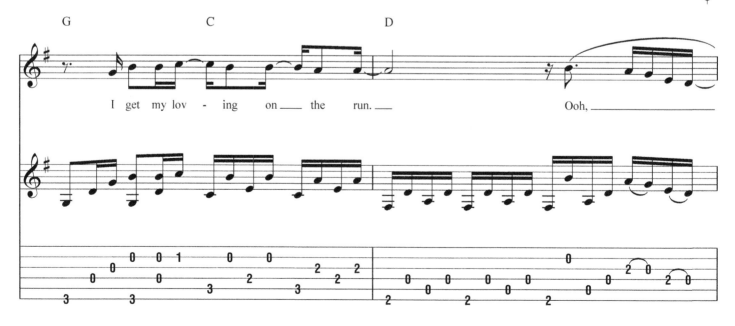

I get my lov - ing on ___ the run. ___ Ooh, _____

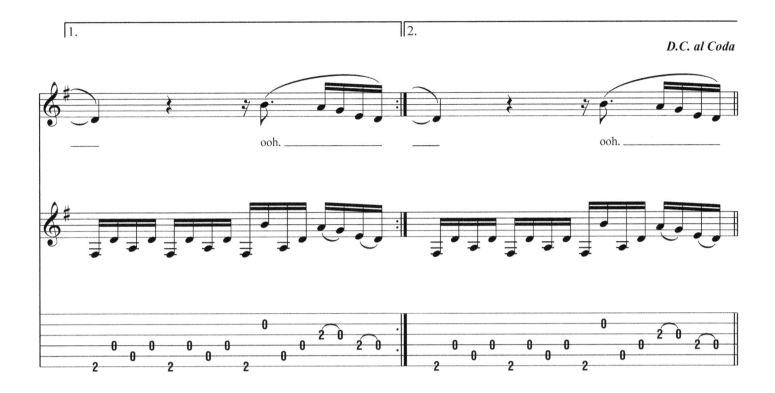

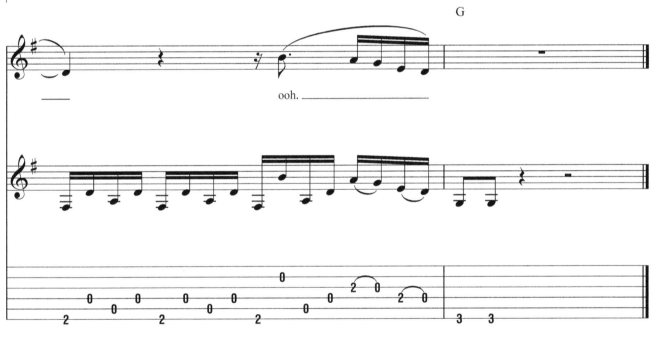

Additional Lyrics

3., 5. You're the cutest thing that I ever did see,
I really love your peaches, want to shake your tree.
Lovey dovey, lovey dovey, lovey dovey all the time,
Ooh wee, baby, I'll sure show you a good time.

4. People keep talking about me, baby.
Say I'm doing you wrong.
But don't you worry, don't worry, no, don't worry, mama,
'Cause I'm right here at home.

Space Oddity

Words and Music by David Bowie

God's love be with you.

Verse

3. This is Ground Con - trol ___ to Ma - jor Tom ___
4. This is Ma - jor Tom ___ to Ground Con - trol. ___

___ you've real - ly made the grade, _____ and the pa - pers want to know ___ whose shirts you wear. ___
___ I'm step-ping through the door. _____ and I'm float - ing in a most ___ pe - cu - liar

Now it's time to leave the cap - sule if you dare. _____
way, ___ and the

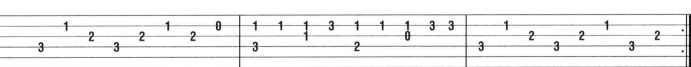

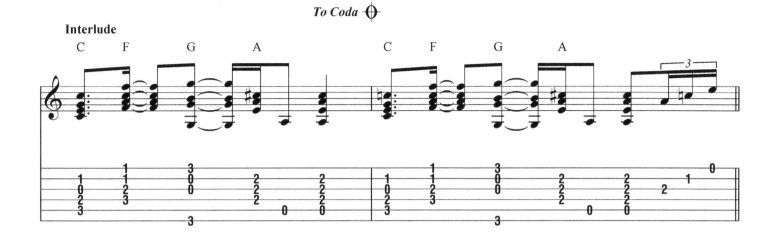

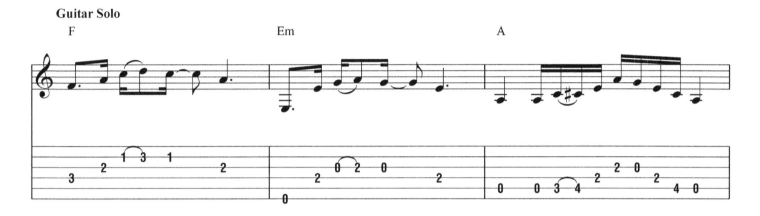

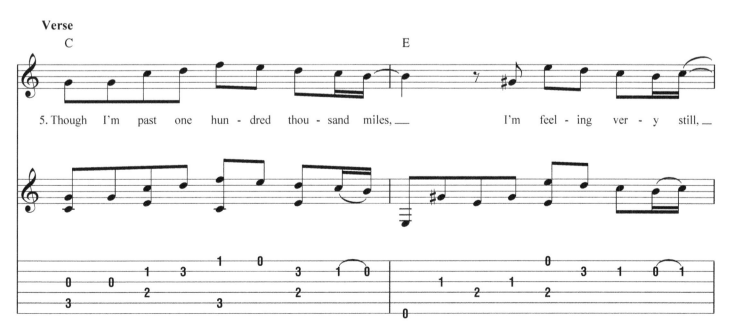

5. Though I'm past one hun - dred thou - sand miles, ___ I'm feel - ing ver - y still, ___

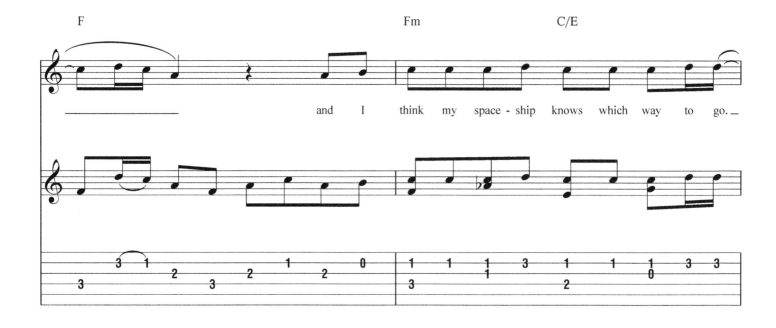

and I think my space-ship knows which way to go.___

_____ Tell my wife I love her ver-y much; she knows.___

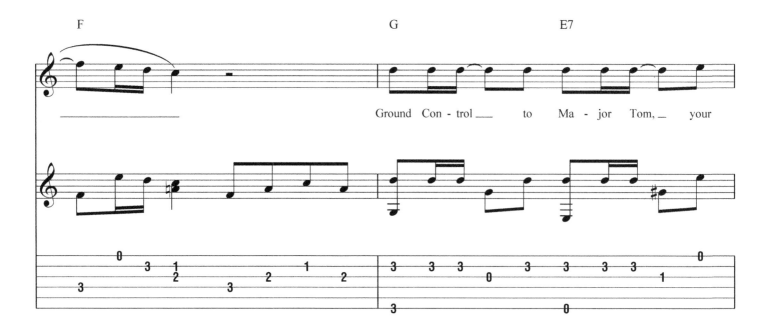

_____ Ground Con-trol ___ to Ma-jor Tom, ___ your

cir - cuit's dead, there's some - thing wrong. Can you hear me, Ma - jor Tom?___ Can you

D.S. al Coda

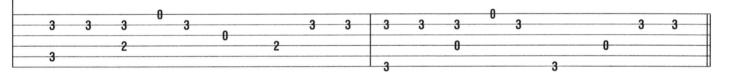

hear me, Ma - jor Tom?___ Can you hear me, Ma - jor Tom?___ Can you...

 Coda

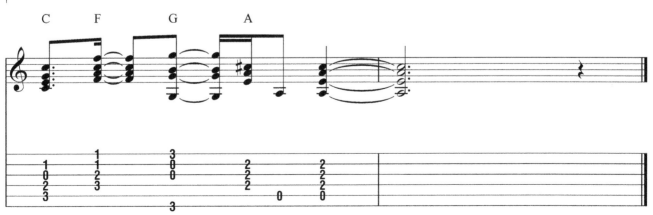

Stairway to Heaven

Words and Music by Jimmy Page and Robert Plant

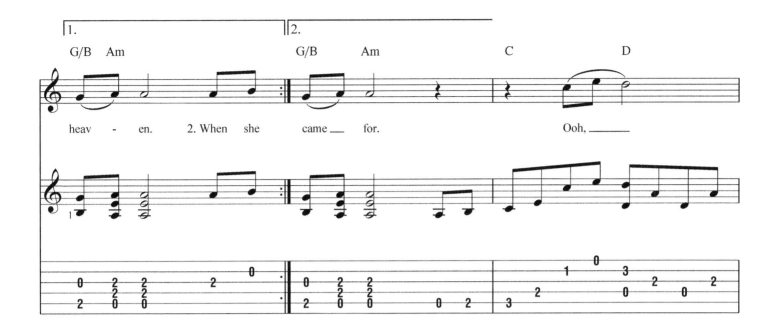

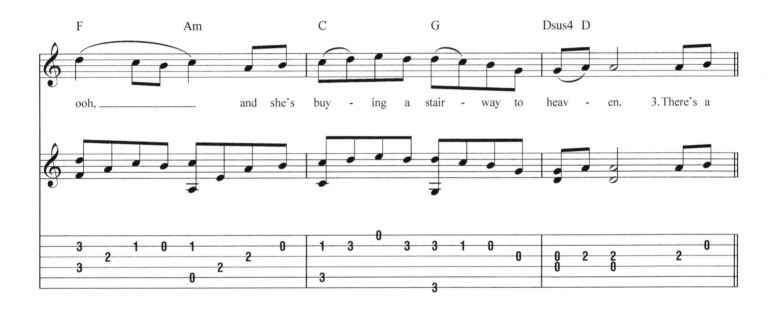

Verse

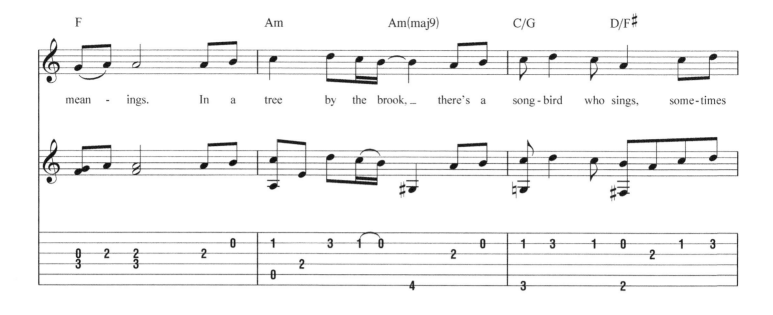

mean - ings. In a tree by the brook, _ there's a song-bird who sings, some-times

all of our thoughts are mis - giv - en.

It makes me won - der.

4. There's a

Verse

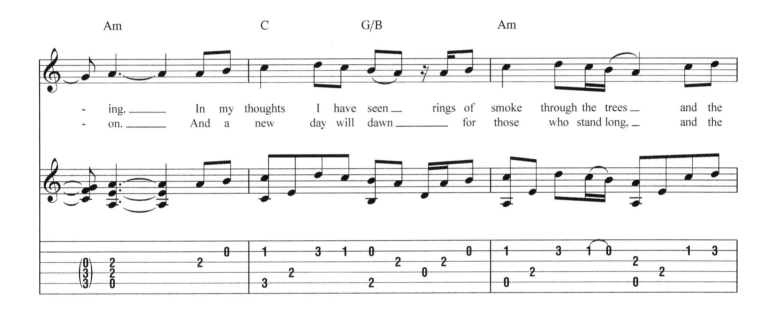

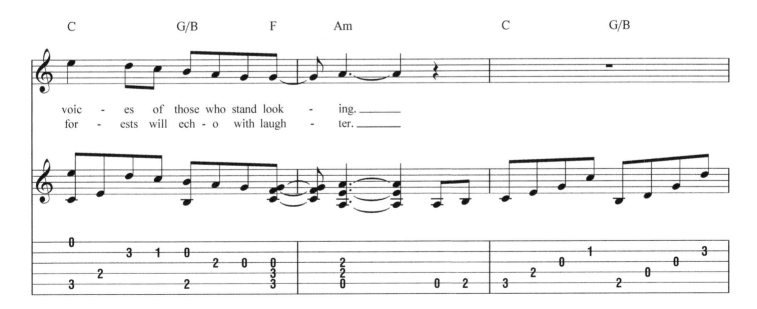

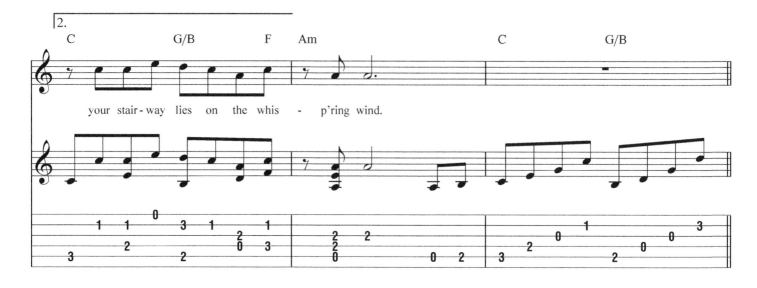

your stair-way lies on the whis - p'ring wind.

Interlude

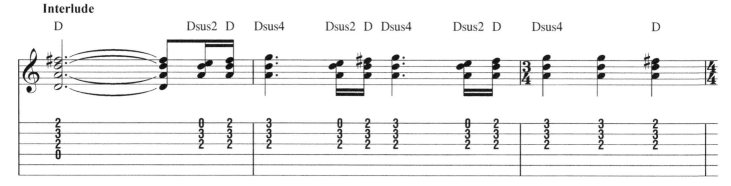

Chorus

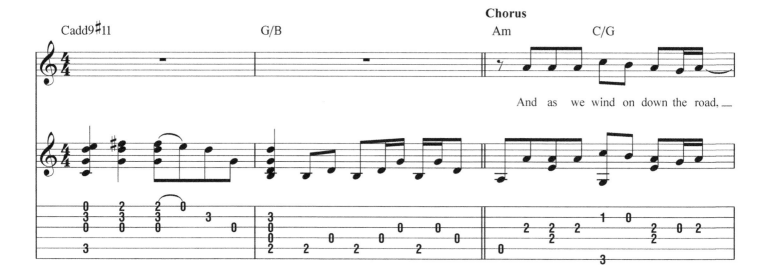

And as we wind on down the road, ___

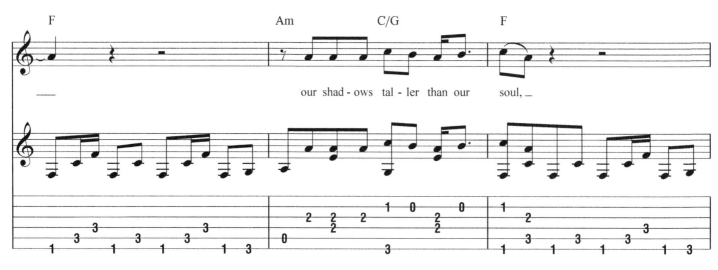

___ our shad-ows tal-ler than our soul, ___

when all are one ___ and one is all. _____

Outro

To be a rock ___ and not to roll. _____

rit.

rit.

And she's buy - ing a stair - way to heav - en.

Harm.

Take Me Home, Country Roads

Words and Music by John Denver, Bill Danoff and Taffy Nivert

old there,__ old-er than the trees, young-er than the moun-
dust-y,___ paint-ed on the sky, mist-y taste of moon-

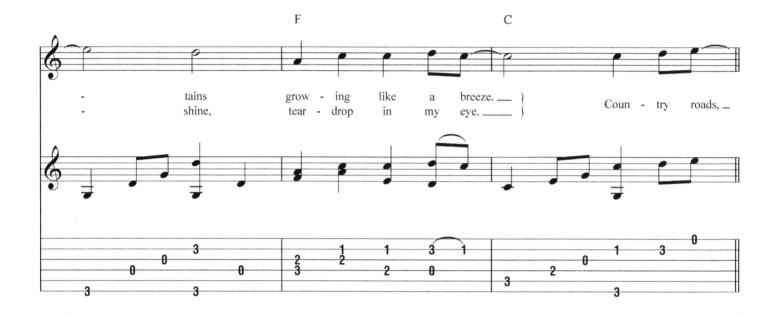

-tains grow-ing like a breeze.__ ⎫
-shine, tear-drop in my eye.___ ⎭ Coun-try roads,__

𝄋 **Chorus**

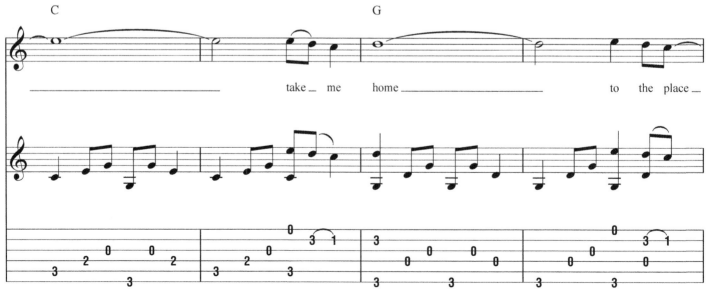

_____ take_me home _____ to the place_

I be - long: _____ West Vir - gin -

- ia, _____ moun - tain mom - ma, _____ take __ me

To Coda ⊕

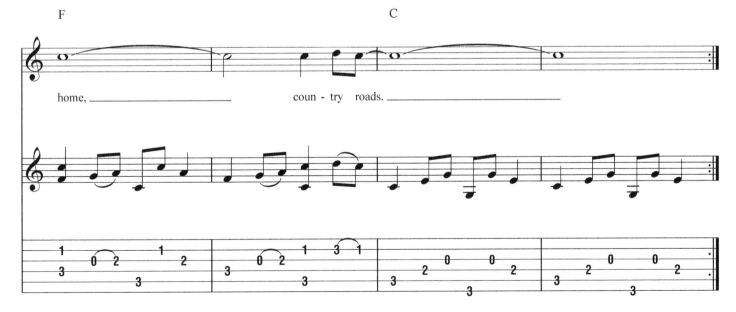

home, _____ coun - try roads. _____

Bridge

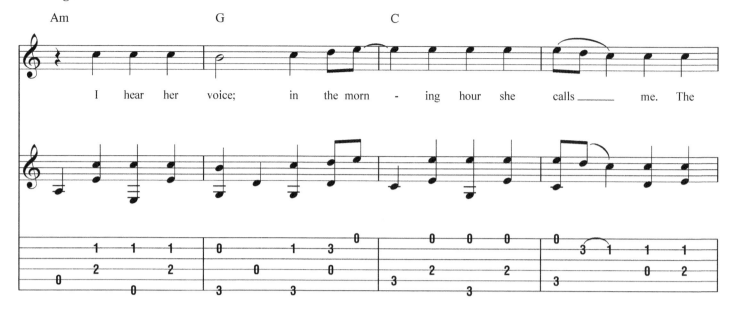

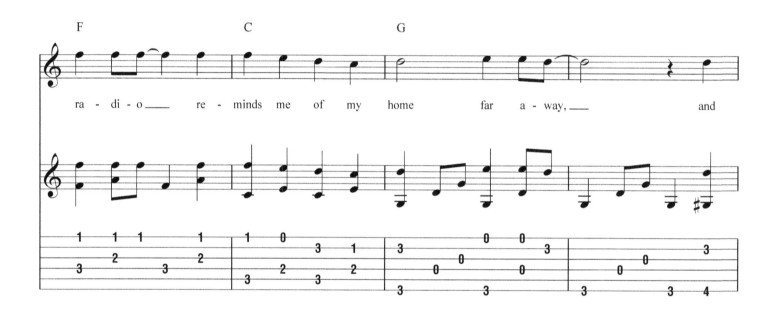

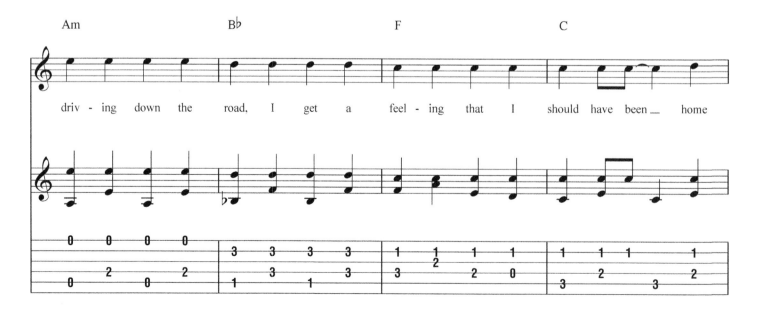

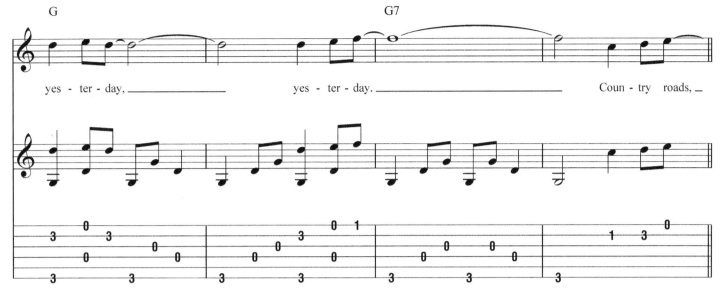

Coda

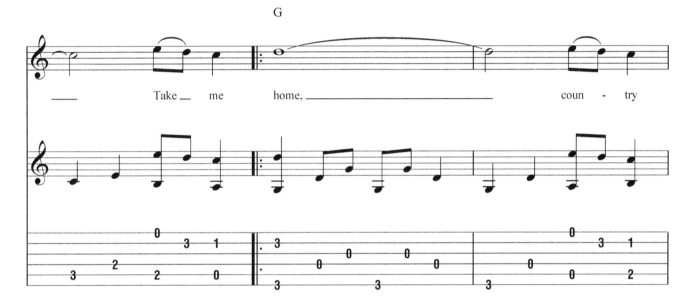

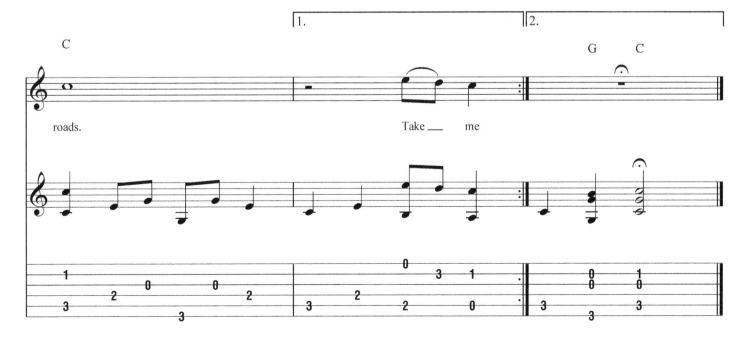

Wild World

Words and Music by Yusuf Islam

I'll al - ways re - mem - ber you   like a child, girl.

Interlude

Verse

3. Ba - by, I love __ you,   but if you want to leave _____ take good

care. Hope you make a lot of nice friends_ out there. But just re-mem-ber there's a lot of bad

D.S. al Coda

Coda

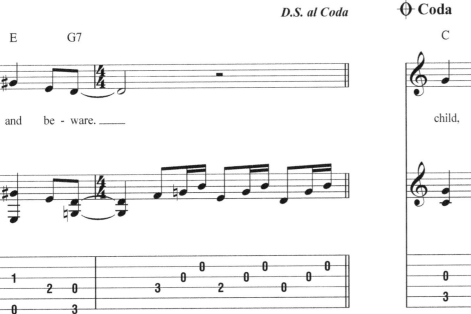

and be - ware._____

child, girl.

rit.

I'll al - ways re - mem - ber you like a child, girl.

rit.

Wish You Were Here

Words and Music by Roger Waters and David Gilmour

Intro
Slow

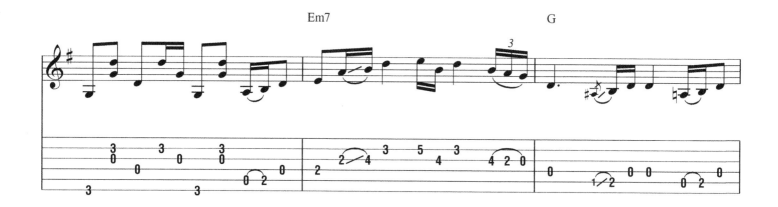

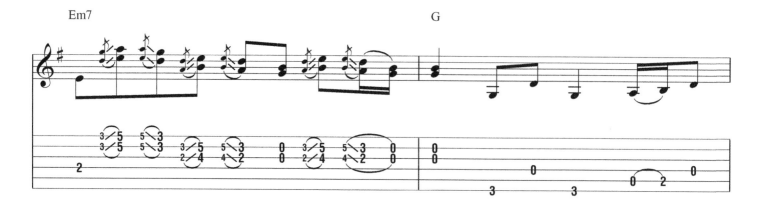

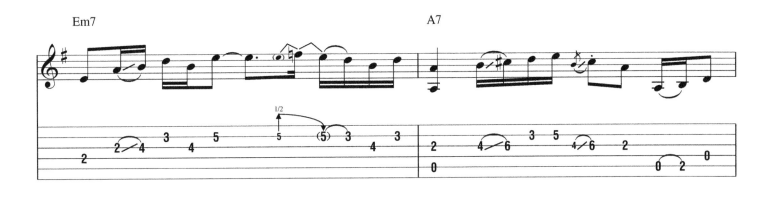

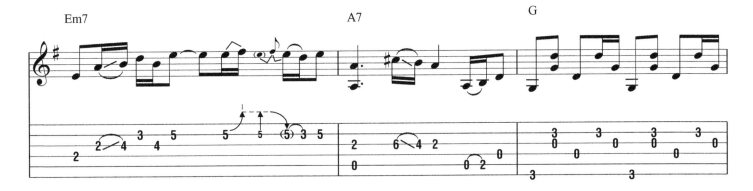

Verse

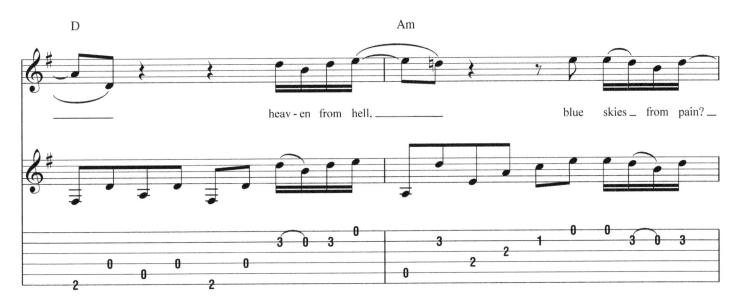

Can you tell a green field from a cold steel

rail, a smile from a veil? Do you think you can tell?

Verse

2. Did they get you to trade your he - roes for

ghosts, ___ hot ash - es for trees, _____ hot air ___ for a

cool ___ breeze, cold com-fort for change? _____ And did you ___ ex - change ___

_____ a walk-on part ___ in the war _____ for a lead role in a cage? ___

𝄋 Interlude

To Coda ⊕

Verse

3. How I wish,_____ how I wish you were here._____ We're just

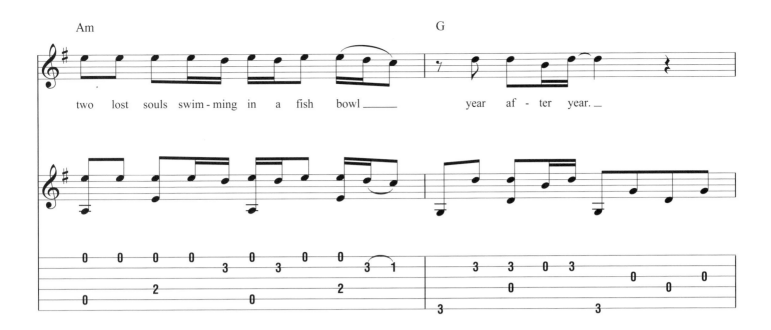

two lost souls swim-ming in a fish bowl _____ year af-ter year. __

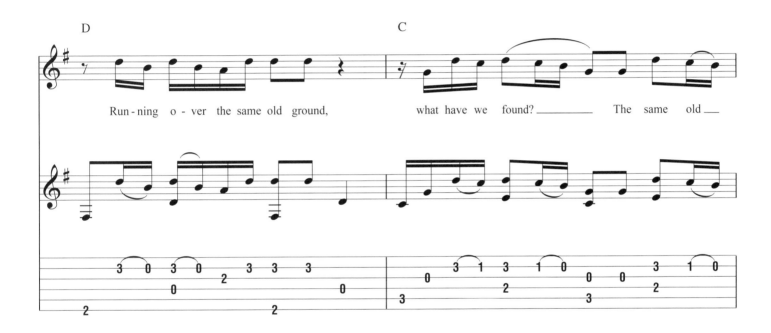

Run-ning o-ver the same old ground,   what have we found? _____ The same old __

D.S. al Coda   ⊕ **Coda**

fears. __   Wish you _____ were here. _____

FINGERPICKING GUITAR BOOKS

Hone your fingerpicking skills with these great songbooks featuring solo guitar arrangements in standard notation and tablature. The arrangements in these books are carefully written for intermediate-level guitarists. Each song combines melody and harmony in one superb guitar fingerpicking arrangement. Each book also includes an introduction to basic fingerstyle guitar.

    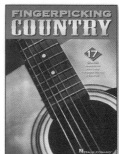 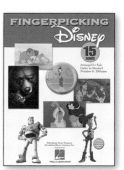

Fingerpicking Acoustic
00699614 15 songs.......................$14.99

Fingerpicking Acoustic Classics
00160211 15 songs.......................$16.99

Fingerpicking Acoustic Hits
00160202 15 songs.......................$12.99

Fingerpicking Acoustic Rock
00699764 14 songs.......................$16.99

Fingerpicking Ballads
00699717 15 songs.......................$14.99

Fingerpicking Beatles
00699049 30 songs.......................$24.99

Fingerpicking Beethoven
00702390 15 pieces.....................$10.99

Fingerpicking Blues
00701277 15 songs $10.99

Fingerpicking Broadway Favorites
00699843 15 songs.......................$9.99

Fingerpicking Broadway Hits
00699838 15 songs.......................$7.99

Fingerpicking Campfire
00275964 15 songs.......................$12.99

Fingerpicking Celtic Folk
00701148 15 songs.......................$12.99

Fingerpicking Children's Songs
00699712 15 songs.......................$9.99

Fingerpicking Christian
00701076 15 songs.......................$12.99

Fingerpicking Christmas
00699599 20 carols.....................$10.99

Fingerpicking Christmas Classics
00701695 15 songs.......................$7.99

Fingerpicking Christmas Songs
00171333 15 songs.......................$10.99

Fingerpicking Classical
00699620 15 pieces.....................$10.99

Fingerpicking Country
00699687 17 songs.......................$12.99

Fingerpicking Disney
00699711 15 songs.......................$16.99

Fingerpicking Early Jazz Standards
00276565 15 songs $12.99

Fingerpicking Duke Ellington
00699845 15 songs.......................$9.99

Fingerpicking Enya
00701161 15 songs.......................$16.99

Fingerpicking Film Score Music
00160143 15 songs.......................$12.99

Fingerpicking Gospel
00701059 15 songs.......................$9.99

Fingerpicking Hit Songs
00160195 15 songs.......................$12.99

Fingerpicking Hymns
00699688 15 hymns $12.99

Fingerpicking Irish Songs
00701965 15 songs.......................$10.99

Fingerpicking Italian Songs
00159778 15 songs.......................$12.99

Fingerpicking Jazz Favorites
00699844 15 songs.......................$12.99

Fingerpicking Jazz Standards
00699840 15 songs.......................$12.99

Fingerpicking Elton John
00237495 15 songs.......................$14.99

Fingerpicking Latin Favorites
00699842 15 songs.......................$12.99

Fingerpicking Latin Standards
00699837 15 songs.......................$17.99

Fingerpicking Andrew Lloyd Webber
00699839 14 songs.......................$16.99

Fingerpicking Love Songs
00699841 15 songs.......................$14.99

Fingerpicking Love Standards
00699836 15 songs $9.99

Fingerpicking Lullabyes
00701276 16 songs.......................$9.99

Fingerpicking Movie Music
00699919 15 songs.......................$14.99

Fingerpicking Mozart
00699794 15 pieces.....................$10.99

Fingerpicking Pop
00699615 15 songs.......................$14.99

Fingerpicking Popular Hits
00139079 14 songs.......................$12.99

Fingerpicking Praise
00699714 15 songs.......................$14.99

Fingerpicking Rock
00699716 15 songs.......................$14.99

Fingerpicking Standards
00699613 17 songs.......................$14.99

Fingerpicking Wedding
00699637 15 songs.......................$10.99

Fingerpicking Worship
00700554 15 songs.......................$14.99

Fingerpicking Neil Young – Greatest Hits
00700134 16 songs.......................$16.99

Fingerpicking Yuletide
00699654 16 songs.......................$12.99

HAL•LEONARD®

0322
279